TAROT
CARDS
COLORING BOOK

MW00946225

MEMORY ACTIVITY BOOK

MEMORY ACTIVITY BOOK

No part of this book may be scanned, reproduced or distribuited in any printed or electronic from without the prior permission of the author or publisher

We love to recieve reviews from our customers.If you had the oportunity to provide a review we would greatly appreciate it. It helps us to continue creating more content so you can entertain yourself even more.

Thank you so much !

THIS BOOK
BELONG TO...

DEVIL

MEMORY ACTIVITY BOOK

THE EMPRESS

MEMORY ACTIVITY BOOK

HANGED MAN

MEMORY ACTIVITY BOOK

THE HERMIT

MEMORY ACTIVITY BOOK

JUSTICE

MEMORY ACTIVITY BOOK

THE EMPEROR

MEMORY ACTIVITY BOOK

JUDGEMENT

MEMORY ACTIVITY BOOK

DEATH

MEMORY ACTIVITY BOOK

THE CHARIOT

MEMORY ACTIVITY BOOK

WHEEL OF FORTUNE

MEMORY ACTIVITY BOOK

THE MOON

MEMORY ACTIVITY BOOK

THE MAGICIAN

MEMORY ACTIVITY BOOK

THE LOVERS

MEMORY ACTIVITY BOOK

ACE OF WANDS

MEMORY ACTIVITY BOOK

ACE OF SWORDS

MEMORY ACTIVITY BOOK

ACE OF CUPS

MEMORY ACTIVITY BOOK

ACE OF PENTACLES

MEMORY ACTIVITY BOOK

THE HIGH PRIESTESS

MEMORY ACTIVITY BOOK

THE SUN

MEMORY ACTIVITY BOOK

THE STAR

MEMORY ACTIVITY BOOK

STREAFET TETT

STRENGTH

MEMORY ACTIVITY BOOK

MEMORY ACTIVITY BOOK

GOOD JOB, YOU'RE ALREADY HALFWAY THERE.
KEEP IT UP !

We love to recieve reviews from our customers.If you had the oportunity to provide a review we would greatly appreciate it. It helps us to continue creating more content so you can entertain yourself even more.

Thank you so much !

MEMORY ACTIVITY BOOK

AND NOW UNIQUE ILLUSTRATIONS

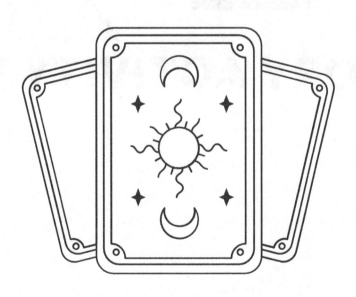

MEMORY ACTIVITY BOOK

MEMORY ACTIVITY BOOK

MEMORY ACTIVITY BOOK

MEMORY ACTIVITY BOOK

MEMORY ACTIVITY BOOK

MEMORY ACTIVITY BOOK

MEMORY ACTIVITY BOOK

MEMORY ACTIVITY BOOK

MEMORY ACTIVITY BOOK

MEMORY ACTIVITY BOOK

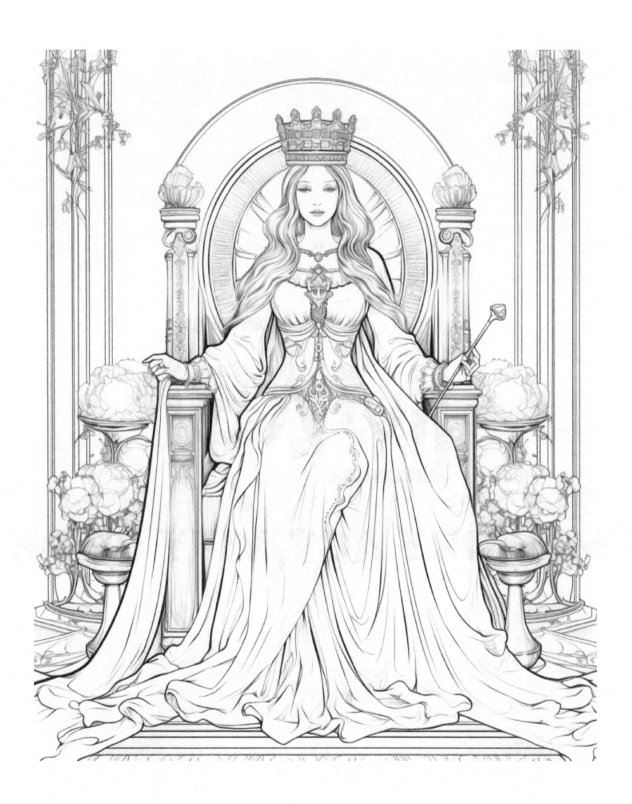

MEMORY ACTIVITY BOOK

MEMORY ACTIVITY BOOK

MEMORY ACTIVITY BOOK

MEMORY ACTIVITY BOOK

MEMORY ACTIVITY BOOK

MEMORY ACTIVITY BOOK

MEMORY ACTIVITY BOOK

MEMORY ACTIVITY BOOK

MEMORY ACTIVITY BOOK

MEMORY ACTIVITY BOOK

We hope you had fun painting with us.
We wait for you in the next Vol

We love to recieve reviews from our customers.If you had the oportunity to provide a review we would greatly appreciate it. It helps us to continue creating more content so you can entertain yourself even more.

Thank you so much !

MEMORY ACTIVITY BOOK

Made in United States
North Haven, CT
14 January 2024

47474260R00050